What Spilled
When
Door of
Was
Left Ajar

Poetry that began in childhood and spilled out across the years of growing up, and growing older.

7- 14 - 2001

To the Hughes... A time for Sharing !

Willard "Bud" Hartshorn

Additional copies available from:
Summit Publishing Company
1256 Summit Road
Cheshire, CT 06410

LIBRARY OF CONGRESS CATALOG
CARD NUMBER 91-65836

ISBN 0-9629603-6

PUBLISHED BY
SUMMIT PUBLISHING CO.
1256 Summit Rd.
Cheshire, CT 06410

FOREWORD

We are constantly adding memories to our lives - fond, joyous, startling, sad. They all form our growth patterns and move us in a direction called life.

That we may be a product of our memories may not be far afield.

As you scan the contents here, notice how close some of my memories reach out to where you were at times. Even as we feel our own uniqueness, we can grasp a sense of oneness, as we visualize what we read in the word pictures that follow!

Dedicated

To my wife and constant companion, as we traveled from poetry reading to poetry reading, listening over and over to words she must know almost by heart, yet never complaining or looking for an out.

About the author

Willard L. Hartshorn ("Bud") was born in Waterbury, Vermont in 1922. He won his first literary award at age twelve in Waterbury, Connecticut. His first volume of poetry was published in 1973. It quickly sold out and is out of print. He has given poetry readings throughout Connecticut and New York. He is associated with the Connecticut Poetry Society, the National Academy of Repertory Poetry, and the Artists and Writers of Connecticut, where he has served as treasurer since 1966. His work with senior citizens in the field of creative writing has been welcomed by OASIS and performed in senior centers around the greater Waterbury area. He resides in Cheshire, Connecticut with his wife, the former Jean Ruda, and their five children, adopted and foster.

About the illustrator

Grace Jenkins Spring is a Kindergarten teacher in the Town of Plymouth (CT) School System. Besides her teaching, she has a particular interest in many forms of art and design. She sings in her church choir and plays in the handbell choir. During her summer vacations she teaches a workshop in creative writing with children in grades two to five.

She is a member of the Connecticut Writers League, Inc. and the CONNtemporary Writers Group.

Mrs. Spring has illustrated THE FURRY WIND, written by Patricia Ryerson Boyd, and THE YELLOW THREAD CAT, written by Mary Anna Tien. She has also written and illustrated THE FABULOUS HOUSE OF MARCELLA MOUSE, MARCELLA MOUSE MEETS MARVIN AND MARCELLA MOUSE VISITS MR. MOLE. All of these books were published by Andrew Mountain Press.

CONTENTS

Foreword	III
Dedication	IV
About the Author	V
About the Illustrator	VI
That You May Know	10
A First Encounter	12
My Mailbox Prison	14
A Wand of Maple	16
Haydust	19
To A Little Boy On A Rail Fence	20
The River	21
Security	23
Book Of Life	24
Afterglow	25
Friendship	26
Instant Of Quiet	27
Twenty-third Anniversary	29
A Simple Bow	31
Twilight Time	33
The Wealthiest Man	35
To The Mother Of The Bride	37
Met In Kiss	39
To My Family	41
'Tis Christmas Time	43
The Dance	46

Our Silver Anniversary   49
Watchman And Father   51
In My Father's House   53
Daisies Don't Tell   56
A New Day   57
Time   59
The Acorn   61
When Roses Say Farewell   63
Where Roses Bloom   64
No Tomorrow   65
Empty Promises, Contentment, Indecision   67
Reckless Winds   68
Wayward Heart   70
Here On An Island   71
Loving Hands   73
To Barb and Dave   74
Night Wind   76
What Are The Words   77
Birch Trees   81
Who Will Finish What We Start?   83
Taps   87
Progress   89
Homecoming   93
In Tribute   95
Saudi Arabia   97
Acknowledgments   99

That you may know

I would not that you should read again
  of what I write until you know it well
But that on reading understand I saw it thus
  and chose this only way I know to tell.
If I should clutter up where every pause
                should fall
  with marks of courtesy along the way
I don't believe that I would have the heart
  to tell you all the things I have to say.
My eyes have held close to them treasures
                rare
My heart heard sounds my ears could never
                know
My being felt vibrations that were
                everywhere
  and I have shaped them up that they may
                show.

The inkprints that you find on pages
here
have formed through years by being
what they are,
Picked up and reset by me for you -
what spilled when the door of life was
left ajar.

A First Encounter

An inky blackness came last night
    and sat upon our lawn.
It covered up our flower beds
    'til everything was gone.
I wondered if the dark was heavy -
    would it bend or break my tree?
How I wished the sun were shining
    so that I might look and see.
Both hands cupped beside my eyebrows,
    forehead pressed against the pane -
All was gone outside my window;
    only cold and dark remained.
Back beneath my covers creeping
    I could hear the family sleeping;
Waved goodnight to Teddy Nite Lite
    on the table near my door.
And this morning with real pleasure
    I retrieved a glowing treasure;

Picked a rose that had not suffered
    by the dark the night before.
Now I know dark is not heavy -
    only cold, and nothing more.

My Mailbox Prison

White crystals raised like ice cream and
they're mine.
They're mine because my mailbox makes it so.
I'll lick some off before the school bus
comes,
Warm tongue will make these crystals go.
This snowy ice has turned to magnet freeze.
How quick it grabs and holds me tight.
How cold it is and as I try to breathe
It pulls and hurts and fills me full of
fright.
I cannot swallow now, nor yet cry out!
With eyes that dart in stabbing glances here
I wish that I could scream or even shout
To anyone who happens to be near.
I do not even recognize my voice -
These choking sounds that from deep down
have risen -

While I am locked on this cold sheet of
steel,
'Til I'm released from this, my mailbox
prison.

In the great depression, the kids of working dads, had toys. When we saw those sleds come bouncing down the hill and heard the shouts of joy from the riders, we were envious to a point. But it caused us to dream up our own moments, even if make believe. We played with non-existent toys, and dreamed of things that could not be - and who's to say if that was good or bad.

A Wand of Maple

In a little old New England town snuggled
   close to wooded hills,
Where forests seemed unscarred as yet
   and town folk loved those rocks and rills,
I stood and traced a magic line
   with a wand I'd cut from maple brush
And tied it with a piece of twine
   as big as the town or almost such.
Then when I'd set this place apart
   from any other I had known

I caused a newer season's start
  to show it was my very own.
I took the wand and caused a rainbow
  to be arched across the skies,
 Then pushed each end toward the middle
  and made a snowball giant size.
 Next I switched the sun on brightly
  with a wave of magic hand.
Instantly was then created
  a different winter wonderland!
I tossed the rainbow toward the sun
  and caused a wintry wind to blow,
So as the rainbow melted down
  there fell a multi-colored snow.
All the droplets seen as water
  or as velvet liquid dew
I changed to be a colored icing
  draped on everything in view.
Then I switched the sun off quickly
  turned the moon on full and bright,
Making ready to go sledding

on a snow that wasn't white.
Here I ride a pinkish pathway,
  now I turn to purple lane,
Weaving into green and yellow
  plowing back to pink again -
On a ride that's packed with color
  in a winter wonderland,
Made by just a little fella,
  with wand of maple in his hand.

Hay Dust

With chin in hands on elbows bent,
I laid my chest across the hay;
And watched a spider quite intent,
On laying cables that would sway-
From wall to wall and then to beam,
Back and forth it went with ease.
Little did the spider dream,
That I was just about to sneeze.

To a little boy on a rail fence

Looking upward toward the ground
    quickly downward toward the sky
Oh how awkward to be found
    posing as a butterfly.

The River

Star kissed water is my river,
   swirling, jumping on its way.
Moonlight touches it so gently
   then lets starlight have full sway.
Where was I when leaping water,
   jumped and traveled all that far,
Then returned to this my river,
   capped with dust from distant star?
If some Milky Way is missing,
   in my river it will be -
Balancing atop the water -
   holding, captivating me.
Though the depths are dark and quiet
   in my river at its floor,
I am sure it must be thinking,
   that it, too, should leap and roar.
When the Milky Way has sprinkled
   star dust on my river's bed,

All the magic of some midnight
   will be swirling 'neath my head.
If I touch the water gently,
   would my fingers feel the joy
 That the eyes behold this moment
   for a young and growing boy,
Or would the magic spell be broken
   and the stars go shooting back,
Leaving me beside a water,
   that is quiet, deep and black?

Security

In the darkness where she slept
   snuggled close to bedtime prayer,
Beside a box in which was kept,
   odds and ends from everywhere,
I paused for just a moment brief
   and touched my fingers to her head.
She breathed a sigh of sheer relief
   and turned another way in bed.
Little hands that held a ball
   and moved in play the whole day long
Were resting now against the wall
   while fingers moved to angels' song
The scrapes and scratches here and there
   that had been gained in hearty play,
Were now exposed to night time air
   and warmth of bed to heal away -
These moments are all gone too soon
   but etched in memory remain.
Security is just a room
   where loving hand erases pain.

Book of Life

O Book of Life, your edges tear my hands.
Still I must know what's on another page,
And like the pebbles slowly turned to sands
You wear me down 'til I'm too weak to rage.
With sand you build what soon you will
                        destroy.
Is this the message that is mine to keep?
You cause the man to wish he were a boy
And give the boy great visions in his sleep.
Each day I look for what you'd have me
                        know.
With eagerness I scan each single line,
And push aside the things that may not show,
To save them for a more convenient time.
Are these what cause the heavy page to
                        turn at last?
In your wisdom write what I should truly
                        know,
That I may understand before my time
                        is past.

Afterglow

I lifted the cover of darkness
    to find a magnificent glow,
Then lowered the cover discreetly
    and turned in that moment to go.
But when fingers have been thus
    illumined and secretly tingle
            with joy,
Who could deprive them this
    pleasure, or who could this moment
            destroy.
I lingered a little while longer and
    sipped of the wine that was passed -
Absorbed of the glow all around me
    and wondered how long it would last.
Now and again there's a question
    as questions will ever appear,
But my heart holds the answer
    completely, and the heart is forever
            so near.

Friendship

Build a bridge of friendship, piece by piece
O'er the span of hours, day-by-day.
Let the line grow longer, never cease.
Seat each in his place along the way.
Salty tears be few and far between.
Keep above the clamor of the throng.
Know that life is not just what it seems
And think of it as mirrored right and wrong.
Then at eventide give thanks for friends
That matter now and will unto the end.

Instant of Quiet

When the wind had stopped and was not
the wind
and yet had not become a breeze;
When most of the force had been gathered in
but the leaves still trembled on all
the trees;
When the clouds all perched in unbalanced
stance,
having stopped so abruptly from hither
to yon
(Some standing on tip-toe just waiting their
chance
to bow and to curtsy and then carry on);
When the cricket in quiet then chose
to remain
with nary a chirp in the corner he held -
This was the instant preceding the rain,
that bowed to the noise of the raindrops
that fell.

Author and wife Jean

Twenty-Third Anniversary

A thought had just occurred to me
  that prompted other thoughts to flow.
In reverie I journey back
  with you a half lifetime ago.
Four albums deep the photos pile
  to jog our sense of mind's recall
And other treasures through the years
  that are not visible at all.
I do not need one album here
  nor any picture from its place,
Etched in mind and heart are treasures
  time itself could ne'er erase.
Look into the mirror dearest -
  I will by your shoulder stand
Is not that a happy couple -
  see him gently take her hand.
As he bends to whisper softly
  things that she must surely know

All is still of hearts and roses -
    see the freshness of her glow.
Is she happy and contented
    as she leans to his embrace
With her eyes closed is she dreaming
    as he brushes smiling face?
I wonder if that couple standing
    facing us could ever know
This is how we would be standing -
    three and twenty years ago!

A Simple Bow

Her hands that lifted me with ease and care
The passing years had taken as their toll.
All the suppleness was gone - now stiffness
there
And pain within the swollen joints grown
old.
I stood beside her chair and watched her
wince in pain -
She wanted just to tie a ribbon in a bow.
Her gnarled fingers tried and tried again
in vain.
In blue eyes tears would form and move and
go.
I lifted up her hand and touched it to my
cheek
To transfer all the warmth that I could
share.
In her new manner neither mild nor meek
She drew it back and moving, left me
standing there.

I followed, with my eyes, her chores
around and near,
Where she did not need to move her fingers
so.
Then bending to the ribbon she'd left
lying here,
I shed a tear, and quickly tied -
a simple bow.

Twilight Time

The sun has dipped behind the hill
And in the twinkling of an eye
All of nature's calm and still;
Yet there's light still in the sky
         It's Twilight Time.
Who can measure this brief span
Of interlude that holds so much
Of everything that's known to man,
Yet comes and goes at nature's touch -
         This Twilight Time.
"Just a prayer at twilight,"
The poet said long years ago.
Is there such a thing as just a prayer?
I wonder if we know
         For Twilight Time.
A painter in the years gone by
Captured in a field of rye
A picture that for you and me
Was labeled "Harvest Time."

The sun was sunken in the west.
Hands were folded at their breasts.
Farmers stood with heads bowed low
Amid the harvest needed so -
        At Twilight Time.
Mothers through the years have known
Babies will be quickly grown
And they in turn be left alone
        At Twilight Time
Summer rain and winter snow
Pile up years; and winds that blow
The pages of the book of life
Continue blowing day and night
And only hesitate to blow
        At Twilight Time.
The sun has gone behind the hill
And in the twinkling of an eye
All of nature's calm and still;
Yet there's light still in the sky -
        It's Twilight Time.

The Wealthiest Man

When I am the wealthiest man in the land
and all of my streams harbour diamonds
and gold;
When a platinum scepter I hold in my hand
and I know no extremes from the heat
and the cold;
When my harem is loaded with laughter
and glee
and music is rendered whenever I call;
When I can have everything my eye shall see-
oh the excitement of gaining this all!
I stand by a stream that reflects stars
like diamonds
and fondle the bedsand that glitters
like gold;
Surrounded by forest as green
as the emerald;
shaded from sunlight not hot and not cold
Here I listen to music that's constantly
sounding

that no one has captured in fullness
thereof
I am conscious of inner and rhythmical
pounding
and know that I stand on a level of love.
That this is all mine there is never a doubt
it is all here before me as close as my
hand.
There is no waiting nor reason to pout.
right now I'm the wealthiest man in the
land!

To the Mother of the Bride

By candle light the pews are lit -
White flowers on the altar lay -
The organ music softly plays -
Our friends walk down the carpet way.
O Hall of Welcome you have seen
No happier group assembled here.
Count not that seemly wistful look.
Ignore that splash of dropping tear.
Now mother of the bride depart -
You cannot linger by her side.
This moment tugs upon your heart -
You swallow hard your tears to hide,
Hark the anthem how it plays.
Listen to the pipes so shrill.
Eyes look back - Here Comes the Bride -
And yet she is your baby still.
How proud her father looks!
She smiles and slows his footsteps down.
Look to the groom - unseen 'til now.
There is his bride, he sees the gown

All else is lost - the music swells;
The crowd would seem to disappear.
The bride has stopped - her hand seeks his,
Her father's full release is near.
"Who gives this woman?" a voice calls out.
It's been rehearsed - the answers fill.
As he takes a backward step,
He thinks - she is our baby still!
With my love I thee endow -
The prayers are said; they both arise.
Their hearts are overflowing now;
A light is shining in their eyes.
In moments short they will be gone;
Together they will seek their home,
A part of you will with them go,
Wherever they shall choose to roam.
O Hall of Welcome, you have seen
No happier group assembled here.
Count not that seemly wistful look.
Ignore that splash of dropping tear.

Met in Kiss

Warm lips that hardly even touch
   but rather brush as noses meet -
A kindling this to light the fires
   and thrill the sense of touch-repeat.
Yes, repeat, and then again
   unhurried lips that will transfer
A feeling gone direct to him
   electrically returned to her.
The magnet draws and draws and draws
   'til there is only one it seems -
Tottering at the very edge
   of all tomorrow's hopes and dreams.
Strong minds moving spinning backwards -
   falling into deep abyss,
Where spirits rush together madly
   as the lips are met in kiss.

Bob   Bud   JEAN   JIM

BARBY   MARY

CHIP

To My Family

If it were within my power to impart,
of all these things I would then
freely give:
To each, a fear within a trembling heart,
that must be forged with strength
as life is lived;
Some sorrow I would hand to each and all
that they might overcome and rise again;
Some bitterness for them to swallow
with their pride
that they might taste the scorn of other
men;
Some hardships they may well feel heaped too
high,
deprived of luxuries for a span of time;
Tears to fill what might be drier eyes,
I would prescribe for this dear group
of mine.

These are the valleys I would place them in
   while pointing to the hills above
               the plain,
Hoping that they all might see the rainbow
   that could not be unless there had been
               rain.

Who has not felt the "thundering silence"
where candles flicker near the altar... or
heard the "silvery blast" of long horn
trumpets played by marble angels high above
the vacant pews... especially when

'Tis Christmas Time

I looked around in quiet where I stood;
  then with my heart held gently in my hand,
I moved toward the altar where all good
  waited for each soul to come and stand.
"'Tis Christmas time," I said beneath
           my breath,
  and time again to kneel where angels pray;
To rise again in feeling new and fresh
  and know the meaning of this hallowed day.
The beating of this heart was louder here -
  the quietness around did make it so,
And with the loudness of this beat I fear,
  the quiet that was here, I caused to go.

My eyes sought out the manger scene
                    portrayed-
  how loud this silence was on inner ear.
How gloriously the long horn trumpets
                    played -
  how urgent was the hush that lingered here.
I turned my eyes to off the manger scene
  and looked beyond, but just a prayer away.
In a fox hole out in Vietnam so near,
  words were being formed as clear as day.
Though lips were moving - eyes were still
                    closed tight.
  I did not have to hear what words
                    were said.
It mattered not to him if day or night
  it only mattered here, alive or dead.
I turned a half a prayer unto the south -
  in a Korean outpost barbed wire stands
Where sentry served with bitter taste
                    in mouth
  and held the fate of nations in his hands.

I raised my eyes and looked into the skies
where bombers roared and angels feared to
play;
Then turning back to where all goodness
cries
I looked again to where the Christ Child
lay.

The Dance

We danced to a tune that was young long ago
And we ended the dance with a swing and a
glide.
There were moments between when the hearts
came aglow
And eyes were all shiny and sparkling with
pride.
The floor was soon covered with feet that
were gliding
While everyone held to the one they adored.
This was the moment when dreams were all
sliding
From memory to memory as music was poured
When the tempo was shifted and music was
altered
And nary a foot would obey the new score
The orchestra quickly with never a falter
Returned to the magic it carried before,

And we danced to the tunes that were young
long ago,
Ending our dance with a swing and a glide
With years in between when all hearts
were aglow
And the eyes were all shiny and sparkling
with pride.

Our Silver Anniversary

With shining eyes and eagerness we stood
  and looked across a threshold that was new,
How could we know how much there is to learn
  in that next breath beyond the words,
                "I do"?
The seasons that we've known with highlights
                here
    were sparked by thoughts that only you
            could give.
My memory now must just recall a few
  of thoughts and things that in my heart
              must live.
Because of you our house became a home -
  a framework holding laughter, tears
            and love,
A knowing sense of oneness that we shared
  each with the other and our God above.
In sickness and in health we leaned alike
  to the direction that we knew to be

The only one that you could understand -
  the only one that was the way for me.
Then children came and added untold wealth -
  a richness that no gold could ever buy,
And we were raised in wisdom one more notch,
  thus given newer goals for which to try.
So now tonight by candlelight we sit
  in celebration of this span of life,
As shared again on paper as you read
  what I must sense you would as I did write.
Take then these silver strands that are
                    of me
This sign of age that all must surely show,
  to you I give of me anew, and now
Again I pledge my life with you to go.
  Take then these sterling words
                our own to share,
Carefully signed by one who knows -
                how much to care.

Watchman and Father

In   the   last   of   the   moments   before   I'm
retiring
the household is quiet except where
they sleep.
I'm making my rounds as a watchman
and father -
counting my blessings and checking
my sheep.
I pause by the bedside where Princess
is sleeping
and peek very quickly inside of her dreams.
Am amazed at the height and the depth
and the grandeur
and recognize princes and fairies
and queens.
Her dream is a dream that goes on into space
where the body is warmed by the billions
of stars;
Where the moon as a mirror is held
to her face,

and she winks very coyly at Venus and Mars.
I cannot contain her within fragile
boundaries;
the princess is queen in the realm of her
sleep,
And I am content to be watchman and father -
just counting my blessings and checking
my sheep.

In My Father's House

From stained glass windows sunlight
                filtered through.
The   organ   played   "This   is   My   Father's
                World".
My puzzled mind dwelt on the Scripture, too.
Was that the trigger that these thoughts
                unfurled?

Eyes on the cross above the altar here,
While sermon droned and bodies shifted
                weight,
I saw a hundred different churches
                all appear
And go again and never hesitate.

O burning question now - which is the one?
My own has come and gone and did not stop.
Does this mean that I am not at home -
That I am of the chaff and not the crop?

Be still my soul, the message is not dim
Look up, my eyes and there the answer see.
Do not these questions go straight back to
                    Him?
Is not this answer plain for even me?

Each of the different churches that I saw
Came equipped with its own different clan;
Each with its own symbols and own law.
Father, You do perceive the needs of man!

With hands outstretched I stand before
                    them all
Eager breath held back that none should
                    know.
I'm sure that I can hear my Father call
And know I cannot move - which way to go?

"Father", I cry, "in which do You abide?
Speak again to me that I may know."

"O troubled heart, why don't you look
             inside?
You are your church, this much you need
             to know."

And now before my eyes a shifting plan -
The church's doors are opened clear
             and wide
Till I can see through each from where
             I stand,
And know it mattered not which one I tried.

The paths from out the back all merge in
             unison,
And as I look along, I view in awe
The Temple that I know to be the One
That makes me be the crop, and not the
             straw.

Daisies Don't Tell

He loves me - he loves me not-
   the daisy petals flutter by.
If daisies knew what I know dear,
   each petal would emit a sigh.
She loves me - she loves me not-
   the daisy petals touch the ground
They seemed to wink as they went by,
   while breezes moved them all around.
Now the stem that held the daisy
   holds a single golden shell.
Unanswered question still lies burning-
   daisies aren't allowed to tell.

A New Day

The night removed its darkest clothes
    and stood in shades of softer gray
Then all the birds at once began
    to herald in another day.
The forest slowly came awake
    as grass and bush began to move
The sentinel gone fast asleep
    stone silent was his challenge, Whoo!

I stirred the coals and added wood
    the coffee then was at its best
And as the sun began its rise
    I saw the edge of heaven crest.
'Til heaven had surrounded me -
    and while I sat upon a log
I moved a single blade of grass
    and touched the beating heart of God!

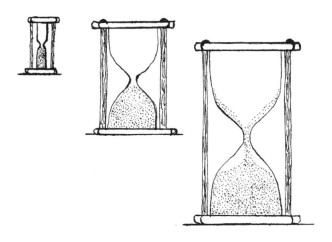

TIME

A rich man cannot buy it
   regardless of his wealth,
A thief can never steal it
   no matter what his stealth.
The idle seldom think of it
   as slowly it drifts by

The busy can't keep up with it
 it moves on wings that fly.
An hour is a minute grown
 a minute is an hour spent
Oh if we had only known
 what was borrowed lost and lent.
The night and day is made of it~
 we all have equal share
Eternity is paved with it
 and we shall end it there.

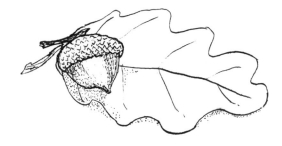

The Acorn

The acorn is a nothing much
    except for squirrels to eat
While it remains an acorn small
    and lies at mortal's feet
But oh the difference we note
    when acorns plain give in
Refuse to be an acorn further
    lets the will of nature win

Down into the warm earth pressing
   letting nature have its way
Sprouting forth its tiny tendrils
   feeding growing day by day
Soon a sapling is seen standing
   what will be a sturdy tree
Another day was just an acorn
   and I turn my thoughts to me.
Am I not just like the acorn
   nothing much just as I am
But should the Spirit move within me
   killing off the carnal man
Nurturing and then transforming
   aiming for eternity
This is then the revelation
   that the acorn gives to me
If I let the acorn wither
   soon the oak tree will be grown
Then will come the understanding
   this is why the seed was sown.

When Roses Say Farewell

The petals close their former spread
　　and just before they slip and fall
They lose to wine their former red
　　and whisper, "I have given all."
Now here I stand where petals fell
　　with feeling deep within the soul
And think I know the story well
　　that roses have no common goal.
When roses speak of love at hand
　　there are not words enough to tell
And who are happy as they stand
　　where at the casket sorrows dwell
As they bear the grief that's sent
　　when roses bid a last farewell.

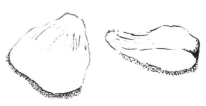

Where Roses Bloom

On moonlit paths where roses bloom
  they stroll in quiet hand in hand.
And when their aimless wandering stops
  the smaller shoes on tiptoes stand.
In solitude a kiss is shared where love
  and lover pause and meet,
And all the noise is swallowed up, that
  comes from off the city street.
The summer air with perfume here
  is isle of magic and recall,
On moonlit paths where roses bloom
  for love and lovers, ages all.

No Tomorrow

What'll we do when there is no tomorrow -
When all our tomorrows are taken away?
All of the things that we'd left till
                    tomorrow
Would still be untouched if today was our
                    day.
We'd look to the list of the memos we'd made
And thrill at recall of the things we'd
                    begun-
Then swallow a lump that gets caught on the
                    way,
And hope to undo all the bad that we'd done-
The unspoken word when needed the most
By a heart that was waiting, so quietly
                    near;
Being contented forever to coast
And fix what needs fixing when goaded
                    by fear.
The day is too short and the list is too
                    long.

Where do we start and what do we do
When all our tomorrows are yesterday's song,
And its spinning and spinning and spinning
                      is thru.

Empty Promises

Here I stand on yesterday's tomorrow,
Making me a liar once again.
O how I wish that I might borrow
A clock whose hands run that way for a
change.

Contentment

Look how that penny now just spent,
Brings the joy of a fulfilled dream;
A smile that angels must have sent,
To the tot at the bubble gum machine.

Indecision

Down a street of broken dreams;
Through a lane of hollow voices;
Here beside a troubled stream,
Are we who made the fewest choices.

Wild Grapes

Do you remember grapes all growing wild
With purple skin about to burst apart;
Sweet and juicy cool and fragrance piled -
When broken open-seeds shaped like
a heart?

*Not long ago the Roman Catholic Church made
some dramatic changes in its' format. The
older generation gasped in amazement and
moved in confusion....They felt enveloped in*

Reckless Winds

We have come up to the edges
    and we waiver at the brink
Looking down on boiling lava
    we can see the edges shrink
Smell the acrid fumes arising
    hear the rumble from within
Just like paper dolls we tremble
    as we bobble in the wind.
All our world is 'round about us
    and it's not a pretty sight
There are those who reach for handsfull
    to be tossed into the night.
But the hands are not yet ready
    for this molten lava here

And the windblown message falters
    where there is no open ear.
There are those who back off gently
    there are those who turn and run
There are those who stand there squarely
    with their eyes into the sun
Blindly standing without looking
    lest they turn in fear and flee
To a place that might be safer
    if that place again might be.
Here is change in form and content
    here is change for change alone
Here is nothing we remember
    here is what the wind has sown.

Wayward Heart

Oh wayward heart - you left a trail
    as sure as violets by the water's pool -
You leaped just like the frog
    quivered like the quail
And left no room at all for head to rule.
You carried like the stream that swept
    and gurgled over polished stones
You ne'er looked back - nor cared who wept
    nor even that they wept alone.

Here On An Island

Each night the sun dips in the sea
  without a splash and disappears
It gives no thought to what will be
  but measures days and weeks and years.

From out the sea the moon comes up
  and drips no water in its' rise
Its' silvery fingers reach right out
  to take the darkness by surprise.

The darkness that the moonlight finds
  is shadow of the things that are
What moonlight deems to do in kind
  is then enhanced by distant star.

How magic is this sparkling show
  that shouts in silence "here am I"
While winking through the afterglow
  at mortal eyes that scan their sky.

From out the sea the journey starts
   into the sea when it is done
Here on an island set apart
   the moon is just behind the sun.

Loving Hands

Fingers entwined but lightly to the touch
  in gentle squeeze slight pressure brought
           to bear
Thumbs move in rhythm and they say so much
  words were meaningless and better rare.
Now heavier beat in veins that both may feel
  held hands pulsate with message from
          the heart
This is a moment all the world would steal
  if they could pry these loving hands
          apart.

To Barb and Dave

There's a quiet in the chapel
   where the saints and sinners meet
There's an awe that is apparent
   as they move on muffled feet
Here the music that is sounding
   is the choice of bride and groom
Let it lift and let it carry
   'til it fills this hallowed room
Let the song that is forthcoming
   be the merry notes that may
Melt the hearts and lift the conscience
   of those gathered here today
Where the hand of love is reaching
   for its symbol or its token
Where the bond of love is welded
   where the marriage vows are spoken
This is island on an ocean
   this is lighthouse on a beach

This is doorway to the future
  with the rainbow out of reach
As you travel toward your rainbow
  hand in hand with heads held high
May the memory of these moments
  be forever 'round and by
And His blessing be upon you both
  where strength and weakness lie.
                With Love - Dad -

Night Wind

Down comes the night wind from on high
  to leave the scattered clouds at bay
Causing trees to moan and cry
  and bend to roughness of his play.
Up from the forest floor the leaves
  are gathered in his playful hands
And taken from the woods as thieves
  would rob and rout a caravan.
The leaves are dropped in meadows near
  and some into the brook near-by
Then night wind with tormenting cheer
  is off again to roam the sky.
His breath directed at the stars
  cause them to flicker blink and nod
Does night wind really move that far
  beyond the earth - so close to God?

Words are a poet's stock in trade - but sometimes in our most diligent search we come up empty-handed; asking ourselves What are the words?

What Are The Words

'Tis said that love is blind
   my love is such
She has been from the moment
   of her birth
Yet gentle hands and fingers
   see so much
How can I know the total
   of their worth.
Could I but just describe
   the color red
Or that color band that's
   arched across the sky
Or even that blue velvet
   that she said
Was going to be her cover
   bye and bye.

The difference in the color
of the grasses
Midday and when they're wet
with morning dew
The way we see a landscape
through sunglasses
And without - the softer
and the harsher view
Now look up - portray this sunset
as you know it best
Leave out the color - and describe it
so she'll see it right
She knows the direction - she can
feel it's west
Feels the warmth of day -
the cool of night
Show her the orange moon
that slowly does appear
And yellow as it gains
a foothold high

Now is white with beams of light
    to blot out darkness here
And keep most lovers looking
    toward the sky
I see all this and just
    because I do
My mind goes racing though
    footnotes of time
In search for words to let
    her see it too
And learn alas - no words
    have been defined.
'Tis I who now am in
    a prison dark
And have no light that can
    be brought to bear
No words to bridge - they all
    are cold and stark...
And darkness waits -
    for beauty to be shared.

The Birch Trees

God sent a silver shaft to earth
from Heaven
it landed where the feet of man
do roam
It multiplied and moved among
the brethren
reminding them of purity and Home.
The birches bend to give to us a
message
we all must bend some purpose
to fulfill
And like the birch send silver shafts
like echoes
that glance through forest thick
or wooded hill.
The birches melt the heart and reach
within us
in regal splendor claim their piece
of sod

In their own way remarkable
and wondrous
converse with man and then in turn
With God.

The B-24 Bombers of World War II were escorted by American Fighter Planes halfway to their target and met again on their return. There were no refueling stops over enemy countries so the fighter pilots dipped their wings in salute and turned back at their break off point.

The following poem deals with the balance of the mission and its outcome. After very few missions of this sort the unspoken question was

"Who Will Finish What We Start"

Winging over cloud formations
  mind a thousand miles away
Catch the shadow of our aircraft
  know we'll soon be in the fray.
Here a bomb-load to deliver
  there a target to destroy
Soon the fighters will be swarming
  in that moment strength deploy.

Tighten up those loose formations
  bring those straggling bombers in
Hold for concentrated power
  this is what will surely win.
Bombers all around us falling
  eager youth about to die
Die because the target's lying
  there beneath this "hell on high"
Parachutes were popping open
  necks were broken by the score
Flaming planes kept spinning downward
  "pull the trigger - this is war!"
Through the intercom comes sobbing
  someone's hit within our crew
Every man must hold his station
  each has got his job to do
Carry on amid confusion
  hope that calm will filter in
Keep your eyes upon your target
  add your clatter to the din
Hear upon the earphones faintly
  bombay doors are opened wide

Feel the air come rushing toward you
  braver men that you have cried.
Who will live to tell the story
  tell it all or just in part
Who will win the fame and glory
  who will finish what we start.
Limping homeward oh so sadly
  with a crew that's hurt - some badly
Wondering if we'll not be hit at least
                    once more
Hoping that we'll clear the mountains
  wondering if we'll make the shore.
The Adriatic Sea behind us
  welcome the Italian shore!
Sweating out another landing
  when the gear's been shot away
Take your landing "Ditch Position"
  now just close your eyes and pray.
Hear the crunch of folding metal
  see the flames go shooting past
Rumbling lurching every which way
  how much longer can it last.

Fire trucks all around us screaming
  stretcher bearers running by
From this mass of twisted metal
  shall emerge a victory cry
Shall emerge from death's own doorstep
  words that never more shall die
Every bomber crew shall learn them
  and shall know them as they fly.

COMBAT CREW 15TH AIR FORCE

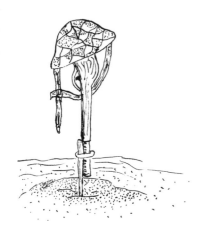

Taps

Day is done . . .
It cannot be for I can see it
               clearly still
I will not let this day go from
               my sight.
Gone the sun . . .
To you 'tis gone but I will hold it
               closer still
And mark the spot wherein I ceased
               to fight

From the lake . . .
From the hill . . .
From the sky . . .
This day is all there is that's mine
                        to hold
And hold it I will try.
All is well . . .
For you 'tis well but what of me
Whose end is here?
Rest in peace . . .
There is no peace where torment reigns
Both far and near.
God is nigh . . .
And I am bowed at last alone.
God is nigh - and peace is still -
A dove to fly - in peril's zone.

*If progress were only rearranging it might
not be as damaging as some of the permanent
types of changes that often occur.
All progress is not necessarily gain.
Sometimes we give up more than we get - and
that can be sad.*

Progress

They stood in awe of woodland
  field and stream
From hilltop viewed the landscape
  sprawled below
Envisioned where the farms would come
  to be
And thought about where school
  and church would go

I stand on hilltop here where once
  they stood
The forest now reduced to
  single trees
The fields now lots where mostly
  flowers grow

And farms and pastures almost
  cease to be.
The houses here are standing
  side by side
They rise and spread that many
  families dwell
Here scars called roads are slashed
  where nature cried
And hardened patches lie
  where soft earth fell.

They drive along on scars across
  the land
And park on scabs above soft
  earth below
To browse in bubbled sores to spend
  their pay
And cast their refuse everywhere
  they go.

When nature cried of rape, they heard
  her not
She shivered long and, sobbed beneath
  their might
She cried aloud and bent beneath
  their will
And prayed for cool and quiet
  dark of night.
Near ravaged to a point of
  no return -
The view that shocks, from here
  atop the hill -
I wonder in these times if man
  can learn
And if he can - I wonder if
  he will!

AUTHOR
1944

Homecoming

Well, I've come - I'm home at last,
  how long I have been gone!
No - there isn't any glory connected with my
                song.
I've been across the ocean - at war in
            distant lands
And now I find myself at home - no blood
            upon my hands
The ribbons here upon my chest were issued,
            more or less.
I'm sure I didn't earn them - no deeds
          do I profess.
I took up my position at the job I trained
          to do -
Behind the guns up in the air - one man
         on a bomber crew.
I went aloft at early morn, and rode
        throughout the day:

To die a hundred thousand deaths when
            hearing "Bombs Away!"
I feared, with all the others, those
            murderous bursts of flak,
And lived through an eternity 'til we'd be
            turning back.
A portion of my job is done - how well,
            I cannot say,
Nor could you judge from over here -
            so many, many miles away.
This much I ask for old time's sake -
            dispense with all the frill.
I do not seek bouquets or crowds -
            that's surely not my will.
To you who know me best -
  for whose presence I have yearned -
Just smile your same old happy smile,
  if you're glad that I've returned.

Mission of January 28, 1986
To the Valiant Seven of Challenger

1 *Dick Scobee*
2 *Mike Smith*
3 *Ron McNair*
4 *El Onizuka*
5 *Judy Resnik*
6 *Greg Jarvis*
7 *Christa McAuliffe*

In Tribute

Through tears we saw what all the world
could see
through tears we saw and did not cry alone;
At this long table seven heroes sat
last meal on earth until returning home.
We saw you walk along in single file
your captivating smiles just held our eyes
Your thumbs-up greeting had just said it all
you entered doors that pointed to
the skies.

We could not follow you to capsule seat
  we parted quickly at the open door
Yours was dreaming - days in space to live
  you could not know the fate that was
              in store.
Ours to count and watch impending doom
  yours to thrill at blue unending sky
Ours to gasp as horror filled our room
  yours to never know the reason why.
Yours the shortest journey into space
  and yet it reached beyond the farthest
              star
To heaven's realm where souls need have
              no face
God knows His own and claims them
              from afar.

On Desert Sands

(Saudi Arabia)

Ancient paths are lighted now by
flares
same paths that camels tread
long years ago
Where bearded merchants traded costly
wares
and moved at paces easy sure and slow.

The wheels that turn inside these metal
tracks
chew sand and spit out dust and flame
Digesting history in minutes flat
designed for nothing but to kill
and maim.
The night sky here now whistles
and it screams
new merchants move at speeds
of quickened breath
Determined merchants, youth
with unfilled dreams
hurtle forth to deal and meet
with death.
Here swirling sand marks history
on its face
and waits return of camels' easy pace.

Acknowledgments

The Waterbury Republican (Sunday edition)

The Cheshire Herald

The New Haven Register

The Salvation Army War Cry

Red Shield Magazine

Stars and Stripes (overseas edition)

Leaves of Laurel

World of Poetry (3) Volumes
  1. Our Western World's Greatest Poems
  2. Our World's Best Loved Poems
  3. Today's Greatest Poems

If you have enjoyed our journey across the years in a somewhat hit and miss approach to the times, it is my hope that you will come back with me and pick up some more of what fell by the wayside.

My next book titled "On Borrowed Time" is already in progress.

Till we meet again,
-Willard L. Hartshorn "Bud"-